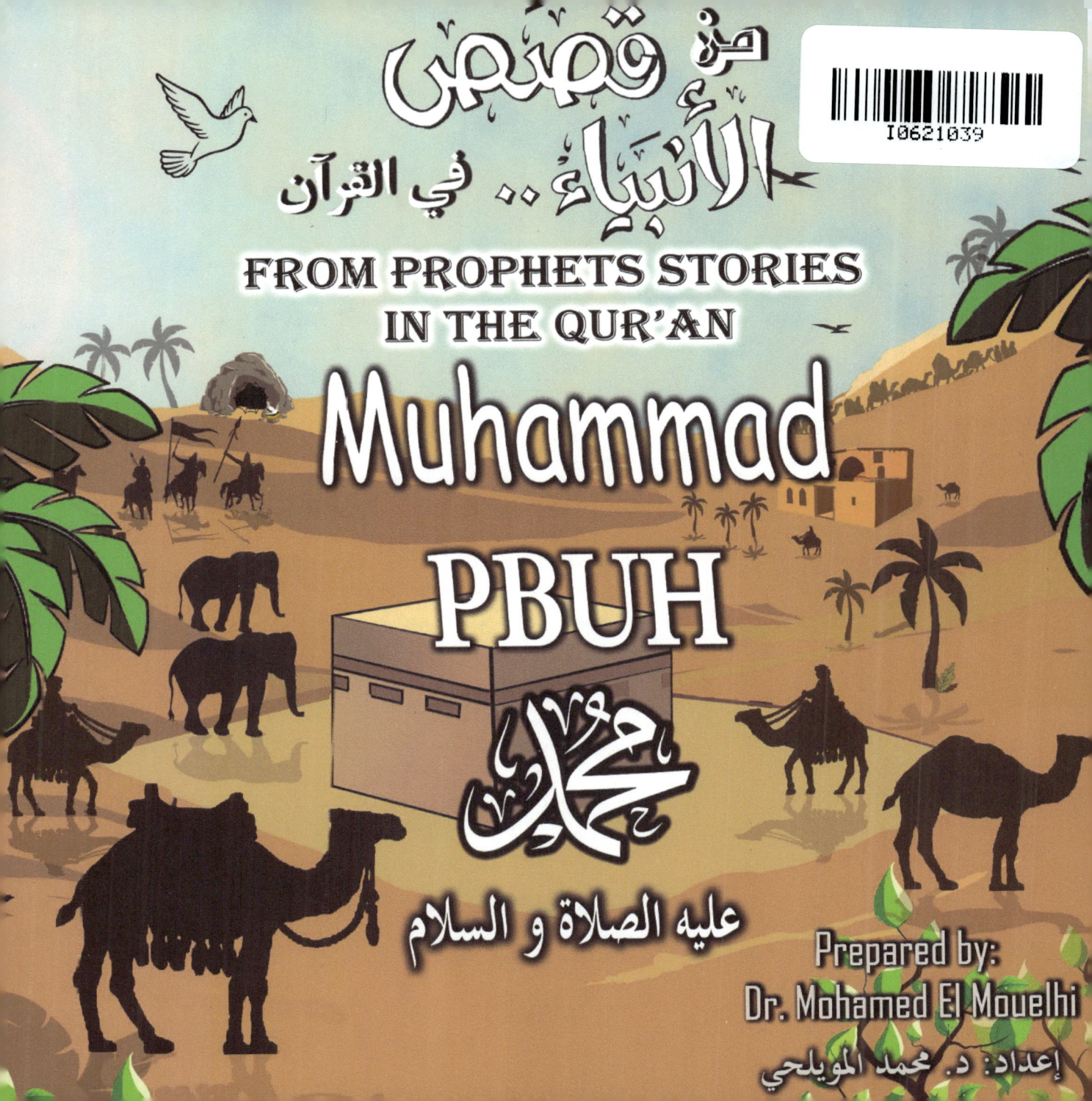

To My Grandchildren, My Inspiration.
-Giddo M.

ISBN 978-1-959536-09-3
First edition 2024

Published by Honey Elm Books LLC
www.HoneyElmBooks.com

Muhammad *PBUH*

محمد عليه الصلاة والسلام

Editing: Noha Elmouelhi

Artistic Preparation: Hossam El Mouelhi

تحرير: نهى المويلحي

الإعداد الفني: حسام المويلحي

MUHAMMAD

PBUH

Prophet Muhammad

(peace be upon him = pbuh)

was born in the Year of the Elephant (571 A.C.)
in Makkah. It was during a time of idol worship
and competition among neighboring tribes.
The year was so named because of an attack on Makkah
by Abraha's Abyssinian army using an army of elephants
in an attempt to destroy the Kaabah (House of Allah).
Allah saved the Kaabah and Abraha with his army was defeated.
The tribe of Quraysh worshiped many idols among which were Allat,
Aluzza, and Manat that were mentioned in the Quran.

ولد سيدنا محمد بمكة فى عام الفيل (571 ميلادى) والذى سُمِّىَ بعام الفيل
لحدوث إعتداء جيش أبرهة الحبشى على قريش لهدم الكعبة مستعملين فيه
جيشا من الفيلة، ولكن الله أباد أبرهة وجيشه وحفظ الكعبة من الهدم. وقوم
قريش كانوا يعيشون فى مكة ويعبدون أصناماً كثيرة، ومنها ما جاء
ذكرها فى القرآن: اللات والعزى ومناة.

1

Muhammad's (pbuh) father,

Abdullah bin Abdul Muttalib,

died before his birth.

Then his mother, Amenah bint Wahab,

died when he was 6 years old.

His Grandfather, Abdul Muttalib, took care of him

until he died 2 years later.

Then, Muhammad (pbuh) was cared for

by his uncle , Abu-Talib.

وقبل مولد محمد عليه الصلاة والسلام توفى أبوه –عبد الله بن عبد المطلب– ، ثم ماتت أمه – آمنة بنت وهب – وهو فى السادسة من عمره، وقد قام جده عبد المطلب برعايته حتى توفى بعد عامين، وبعدها كفله عمه أبو طالب الذى قام بتربيته ورعايته.

Prophet Muhammad
was raised in a community filled
with many temptations.
But Allah protected him and he grew up to be kind
and pure.
Muhammad began his life by tending
sheep to earn his livelihood as was the tradition for the young
generation.
He learned from this job many important lessons such as
patience, mercy, care, and responsibility.

وقد نشأ سيدنا محمد فى مجتمع ملئ بالمغريات، ولكن الله حفظه، وشبّ
على الفطرة والنقاء. وبدأ محمد عليه السلام حياته برعاية الأغنام – كعادة
صغار السن من قومه – ليكتسب رزقه، وتعلم منها صفات كثيرة
مثل الصبر والرحمة والرعاية والمسئولية.

Later on,
he began trading with his uncle Abu Talib.
Prophet Muhammad was called
"The Truthful and Honest One"
because of his trustworthiness and honesty.
A noble woman from Quraysh named Khadija
(may Allah be pleased with her, Aph)
heard about his honesty, and hired him to trade on her behalf.
Her business was very successful, and her admiration
for Muhammad's personality increased.
After some time, they got married and had four daughters.

بعد عدة سنوات اتجه محمد إلى ممارسة التجارة مع عمه أبو طالب، وقد لُقب
بالصادق الأمين لنزاهته وأمانته، وعندما سمعت سيدة من أشراف قريش
وهى السيدة خديجة رضى الله عنها —عن أمانته وصدقه طلبت منه
أن يباشر تجارتها. وربحت تجارتها وازداد إعجابها بشخصية محمد، ثم
تزوج محمد من السيدة خديجة ورزقا بأربعة بنات.

'Did not He find you an orphan
and gave you a shelter (6)
and find you lost, so He guided you (7)
and found you a needy, so He made you rich? (8)'
(Al-Duha)

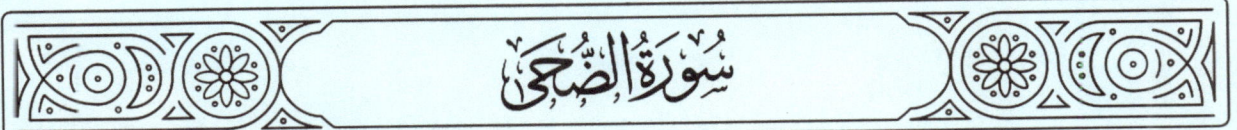

بِسْمِ اللَّهِ الرَّحْمَٰنِ الرَّحِيمِ

أَلَمْ يَجِدْكَ يَتِيمًا فَآوَىٰ ۝ وَوَجَدَكَ ضَالًّا فَهَدَىٰ ۝
وَوَجَدَكَ عَائِلًا فَأَغْنَىٰ ۝

Muhammad used to wonder about the creation
of the Heavens and the Earth.
He used to go alone to the Cave of Hira near Makkah
to meditate.
At the age of 40, the age of intellectual maturity,
Angel Jibril (Gabriel) came down to Prophet Muhammad
while he was meditating in the cave of Hira and revealed the first
verse of the Quran.

وكان محمد كثير التأمل فى خلق السماوات والأرض، وكان يحب أن يختلى
بنفسه بغار حراء قرب مكة ليتفكر فيما حوله وللعبادة، ولما بلغ سن
النضج الفكرى -وهو الأربعين- نزل عليه الملك جبريل وهو يتعبد
فى غار حراء، ونزلت عليه أول آية من القرآن.

' "Read! In the Name of your Lord, Who has created (all that exists)," (1)'
(Al-Alaq)

سُوْرَةُ الْعَلَق

بِسْمِ اللهِ الرَّحْمٰنِ الرَّحِيْمِ

اقْرَأْ بِاسْمِ رَبِّكَ الَّذِىْ خَلَقَ ۝

Muhammad returned home full of doubt
and worry after this unusual event,
and his wife Khadija comforted
him after hearing his story.
Jibril told Muhammad that Allah has chosen him
as His Messenger to call his people to worship only Allah.
Khadija was the first person to believe in his Message. He
began inviting people to Islam in secret, and the first man
to believe in his noble call was his friend Abu Bakr.
Ali Bin Abu-Talib, the Prophet's cousin,
was the first child to accept Islam
at the age of 10.

عاد محمد الى بيته وهو يتصبب عرقاً من هول المفاجأة، وقص
على زوجته خديجة ما حدث له بالغار فطمأنته وكانت
أول من آمن برسالته. بدأ محمد دعوته للإسلام سراً، وكان أول
من آمن به من الرجال هو صديقه أبو بكر، وكان
إبن عم الرسول – على بن أبى طالب – أول الغلمان الذين آمنوا
بنبوة محمد وهو فى العاشرة من عمره.

Muhammad's call to believe in Allah
was met with denial even by his closest family,
including his uncle Abu Lahab and his cousin Abu Sufyan.
Abu Lahab was very hostile and one of the most aggressive
non-believers of Quraysh towards Muhammad
and his followers.
Abu Lahab's wife used to throw thorns and waste in the way
of the Prophet to harm him.
Allah promised His severe punishment for both
Abu Lahab and his wife.

قوبلت دعوة محمد للإيمان بالله بالتكذيب حتى من أقرب الناس إليه ومنهم عمه أبو لهب وإبن عمه أبو سفيان، وكان أبو لهب شديد العداء لمحمد ومن أشد كفار قريش ضرراً بمحمد واتباعه، وقد كانت زوجة أبي لهب تضع الأشواك والمخلفات في طريق النبي للإضرار به، وقد أنذر الله العقاب الشديد لكل من أبي لهب وزوجته.

His uncle and guardian Abu Talib
protected him from the hostility of Quraysh
and prevented them from harming him.
Muhammad loved him very much. He called him to Islam
several times, but his uncle did not accept Islam.
Abu Talib died in the tenth year of the mission.
In the same year, his wife Khadija (Aph) passed away,
which added to the Prophet's grief.
This year was called the Year of Sorrow.

12

كان عمه وكفيله أبو طالب يحمي النبي من عداوة قريش
ويمنعهم من الإضرار به، وكان محمد يحبه كثيرا وقد دعاه للإسلام
عدة مرات ولكنه لم يسلم حتى مات فى العام العاشر من البعثة، وحزن محمد
حزنا شديدا على وفاة عمه. وفى نفس العام توفيت زوجته
السيدة خديجة رضى الله عنها مما زاد من حزن النبى، وسمى هذا العام بعام الحزن.

Allah did not leave His Prophet
in this state of great sadness for long.
He granted him the journey of Isra and Miraj
to cheer him up.
This journey started from Makkah to Jerusalem, where Prophet
Muhammad had the honor of leading the prayer with the rest
of the prophets.
Then, Jibril ascended with him to the seventh heaven, whereby
Prophet Muhammad continued his journey to Sidrat al-Muntaha.
During this journey Allah ordained the prayer for Muslims.

لم يترك الله نبيه فى هذه الحالة من الحزن الشديد فأعد له رحلة الإسراء والمعراج
للتخفيف عنه، وقد بدأت رحلة الإسراء من مكة الى بيت المقدس
حيث صلى محمد عليه السلام هناك ببقية الأنبياء إماماً لهم، وبعدها بدأت
رحلة المعراج حيث صعد به جبريل الى السماءِ السابعة
ثم سدرة المنتهى، وفى هذه الرحلة فرض الله الصلاة
على المسلمين.

14

`Glorified is Allah Who took His slave for a journey by night from Al-Masjid al-Haram to Al-Masjid al-Aqsa, around which We have blessed, in order to show him of Our signs(1).'

(Al-Israa)

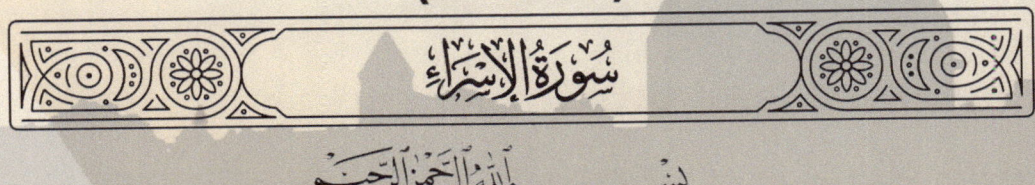

سُبْحَٰنَ ٱلَّذِىٓ أَسْرَىٰ بِعَبْدِهِۦ لَيْلًا مِّنَ ٱلْمَسْجِدِ ٱلْحَرَامِ إِلَى ٱلْمَسْجِدِ ٱلْأَقْصَا ٱلَّذِى بَٰرَكْنَا حَوْلَهُۥ لِنُرِيَهُۥ مِنْ ءَايَٰتِنَآ إِنَّهُۥ هُوَ ٱلسَّمِيعُ ٱلْبَصِيرُ ۝

The hostility of the non-believers against
the Muslims and their torture intensified
in order to revert them back to idol worship.
The Prophet called on the believers to be patient
and to have strong faith in Allah.
In the thirteenth year of the mission, Allah allowed the
Muslims to migrate from Makkah to Medina.
The non-believers of Quraysh became angry fearing
Muhammad's exit from Makkah and the spread
of his message and decided to kill him.
At this stage, Allah allowed His Prophet too
to migrate to Medina.

إشتدت عداوة الكفار للمسلمين وازداد تعذيبهم لهم ليردوهم إلى عبادة الأصنام، وكان النبي يدعو المؤمنين الى الصبر والاستعانة بإيمانهم، وفي العام الثالث عشر للبعثة سمح الله للمسلمين بالهجرة من مكة الى المدينة، وإزداد غضب كفار قريش خوفاً من خروج محمد من مكة وإنتشار دعوته، فقرروا القضاء عليه، وعندها أذن الله لنبيه بالهجرة للمدينة.

The non-believers knew of Muhammad's intention to migrate to Medina.

They plotted to kill him and waited in front of his house.

Allah informed His Prophet Muhammad of their plan, so Ali bin Abu Talib slept in Muhammad's bed to trick them.

With Allah's help, Prophet Muhammad was able to escape without being seen.

He began his migration to Medina with his friend and trusted companion Abu Bakr.

عرف الكفار بنية محمد للهجرة الى المدينة فتربصوا أمام بيته منتظرين خروجه لقتله، وأخبر الله نبيه محمد بخطتهم، فطلب محمد من إبن عمه على بن أبي طالب أن ينام فى فراشه وبذلك يظن الكفار أنه نائم فى الفراش، وقد تمكن محمد بعون الله من المرور أمامهم دون أن يروه، وبدأ هجرته الى المدينة مع صديقه الوفى أبو بكر.

19

Quraysh were very angry
when they discovered Muhammad had escaped.
They went in search of him and arrived
at the cave of Thawr on the outskirts of Makkah while
Muhammad and Abu Bakr were hiding inside.
Abu Bakr was saddened by the situation,
but Allah's Messenger assured him that Allah was with them
and He would protect them.

جن جنون قريش عندما اكتشفوا فرار محمد، فانطلقوا وراءه حتى وصلوا
الى غار ثور وهو فى الطريق الى المدينة وكان محمد وأبو بكر بداخله. وحينها
شعر أبو بكر بالحزن الشديد لعدم قدرته على توفير الحماية
اللازمة للرسول، فطمأنه الرسول بأن الله معهما وأنه سيحفظهما.

`...when they were in the cave,
and he said to his companion: "Don't be sad,
surely Allah is with us ..." ' (40)
(Al-Tawba)

سُورَةُ التَّوۡبَةِ

بِسۡمِ ٱللَّهِ ٱلرَّحۡمَٰنِ ٱلرَّحِيمِ

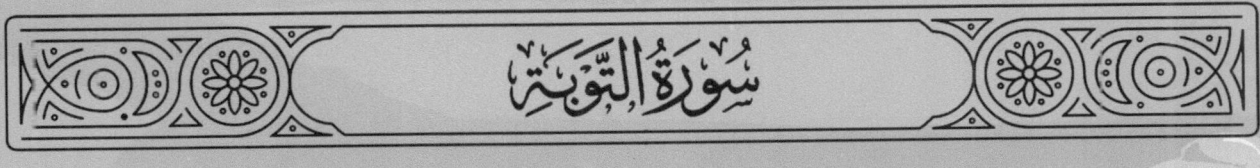

...إِذۡ هُمَا فِى ٱلۡغَارِ إِذۡ يَقُولُ لِصَٰحِبِهِۦ
لَا تَحۡزَنۡ إِنَّ ٱللَّهَ مَعَنَا... ﴿٤٠﴾

This was a challenging
and dangerous situation;
would Allah abandon His Prophet?
The non-believers stood in front of the cave entrance
searching for Muhammad and his companion.
They found a bird's nest and a spider web blocking
the entrance, so they didn't go inside.
They thought that surely no one could have entered recently with
both of these creatures' homes being undisturbed.
Allah saved His Prophet and his friend.

هذا موقف خطير وحرج، فهل سيتخلى الله عن رسوله؟ بالطبع لا... وقف
الكفار الباحثون عن محمد وأبو بكر أمام باب الغار، فرأوا عش
حمامة وخيوط عنكبوت على مدخل الغار مما يجعل دخول أى
شخص مستحيل، فانصرفوا بدون دخول الغار. ونجا محمد
وصديقه وواصلا هجرتهما للمدينة.

Muhammad and Abu Bakr
arrived safely in Medina.
The people of Medina welcomed Muhammad
and the others who emigrated.
He established a brotherhood between the people
of Medina - the "Ansar" (i.e. the Prophet's supporters) -
and the emigrants from Makkah – the "Muhajirun".
Quraysh became increasingly angry and fearful
of the spread of Islam.
They put in place economic sanctions against the Muslims and
prevented the neighboring tribes from trading with the Muslims.

رحب أهل المدينة برسول الله والمهاجرين معه، وآخى الرسول بين أهل
المدينة الذين عرفوا بالأنصار لمناصرتهم لرسول الله وبين
المهاجرين من مكة. وازداد غضب قريش وخوفهم
من إنتشار دعوة محمد، فقاموا بالتضييق على المسلمين
بمنع القبائل المجاورة من التجارة مع المسلمين.

23

As a result of the economic sanctions
and the migration of Muslims from Makkah
without their wealth, life became very difficult
for the Muslims.
They tried to intercept a Quraysh caravan full
of goods and to divert it to Medina.
But the convoy managed to escape and arrived safely
in Makkah.

ضاق الأمر بالمسلمين نتيجة لمنع التجارة معهم وفقد المهاجرين لكل
ممتلكاتهم التى تركوها بمكة، وعرف المسلمون بمرور قافلة لقريش
محملة ببضائع كثيرة، فقرروا إعتراضها وتحويلها الى المدينة، ولكن
القافلة إستطاعت الفرار ووصلت سالمة إلى مكة.

Quraysh considered this caravan
interception attempt as hostile, and they
prepared to fight the Muslims.
The two armies met near Badr in the second year
of Hijrah in what came to be called the Battle of Badr.
Quraysh's army was three times the size of the Muslim army,
but with Allah's Help, the Muslims defeated
the non-believers.

اعتبرت قريش هذه المحاولة شرارة حرب مع المسلمين، وقاموا بإعداد
العدة لمحاربة المسلمين. وقد تقابل الجيشان قرب بدر في العام الثاني من
الهجرة بما عرف بغزوة بدر، وكان عدد جيش قريش ثلاثة أضعاف
جيش المسلمين، ولكن بعون الله انتصر المسلمون على الكفار.

After their defeat at Badr,
Quraysh prepared an army of three thousand
fighters for revenge.
They advanced to Medina in the third year of Hijra.
The Muslims decided to go out to meet the non-believers
at Mount Uhud with an army one third the size
of Quraysh's army.

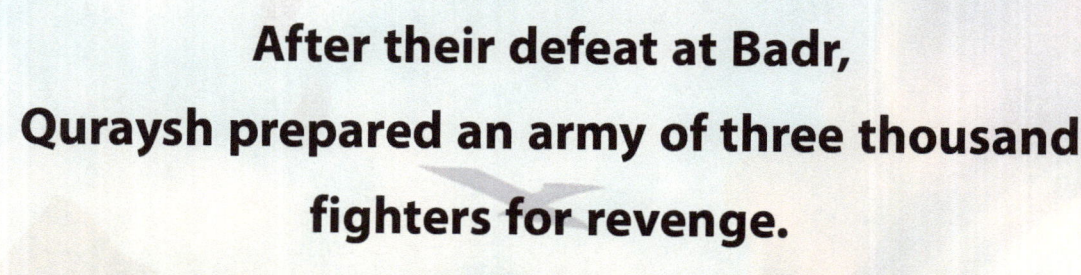

وبعد الهزيمة في بدر أعدت قريش جيشاً كبيراً من ثلاثة آلاف مقاتل للإنتقام، وتقدم جيش قريش نحو المدينة في العام الثالث الهجري، وقرر المسلمون الخروج للقاء الكفار عند جبل أحد وكان عددهم ثلث عدد جيش الكفار.

On the way, a third of the Muslim
army withdrew! The Prophet strategically arranged
the Muslim army and placed a group of archers
at the top of Mount Uhud to protect the Muslim army's rear.
He stressed to the archers that they were not to leave their post
under any circumstances.
The Muslims killed many of the non-believers, who soon
began to withdraw.
Some of the archers thought that the battle was over and left
their post at the top of the mountain to collect
the rewards from the battle.

وفى الطريق انسحب ثلث جيش المسلمين! وقام الرسول بترتيب جيش المسلمين
ووضع فرقة من الرماة على قمة جبل أحد لحماية ظهر المسلمين، وشدد
عليهم بعدم ترك مواقعهم تحت أى ظرف. وبدأ القتال وقام المسلمون
بقتل كثير من المشركين، وبدأ المشركون فى الإنسحاب، وعندها
ظن بعض الرماة أن المعركة إنتهت فتركوا مواقعهم فوق
الجبل لجمع الغنائم.

One of the Quraysh leaders
- Khalid bin Al-Walid before embracing Islam -
saw this golden opportunity.
With the archers gone, he led his troop from behind
the mountain and was able to successfully
attack the Muslims.
The Muslims were defeated because they disobeyed
the orders of their leader Prophet Muhammad.

فرأى أحد قواد قريش –خالد بن الوليد قبل اعتناقه الإسلام – هذه الفرصة الذهبية
فقام بالإلتفاف من خلف الجبل مع فرقته وداهم المسلمين، وانهزم المسلمون
لمخالفة أوامر قائدهم.

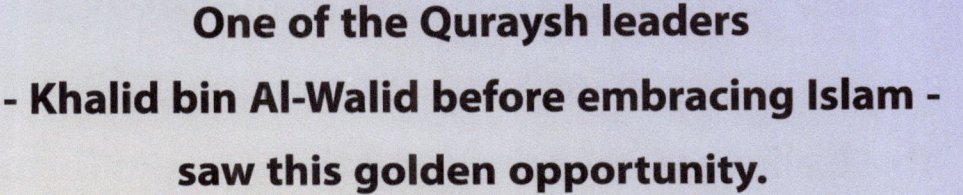

29

In the sixth year of migration,
the Prophet saw in a dream that he was
performing Umrah.
The believers prepared to travel to perform
Umrah with the Prophet.
When they arrived at Al-Hudaybiyah, news came
that Quraysh were preparing to prevent the Muslims
from entering Makkah.
Quraysh sent a representative to negotiate with Muhammad.
The two parties signed the treaty of Hudaybiyah,
which stipulated the establishment of a truce for
a period of ten years between the two parties
and that the Muslims would return the following
year for Umrah.

وفى السنة السادسة للهجرة رأى النبى فى منامه أنه يؤدى
العمرة بمكة، فاستعد المؤمنون لأداء العمرة مع النبى. وعندما وصل المؤمنون
الى الحديبية جاءت أخبار أن قريش يستعدون لمنع المسلمين من دخول مكة، وأرسلت
قريش مندوباً لها للتفاوض مع محمد. واتفق الطرفان على صلح الحديبية والذى يقضى
بإقامة هدنة لمدة عشر سنوات بين الطرفين وأن يعود المسلمون العام التالى للعمرة.

After the Prophet
and the Muslims returned to Medina,
Quraysh broke the treaty by helping one of the tribes
hostile to the Muslims.
Muhammad prepared a large army of Muslims (12,000 fighters)
to conquer Makkah and discipline Quraysh
for breaking the treaty.
Makkah was conquered with Allah's help.

وبعد عودة الرسول عليه الصلاة والسلام ومن معه الى المدينة نقضت قريش الصلح بمساعدتها لأحد القبائل المعادية للمسلمين، فجهز رسول الله جيشاً كبيراً من المسلمين (12 ألف مقاتل) وتوجه الى مكة لفتحها ولعقاب قريش، وتم فتح مكة بعون الله.

After the conquest of Makkah,
there were a large number
of prisoners from Quraysh.
The Messenger of Allah asked them what they thought
would become of them?
The prisoners, fearing Muhammad's revenge,
replied, "To be treated with kindness, O generous man
and son of a generous man."
So the Messenger of Allah freed them.
Glory be to Allah, who bestowed upon His Prophet
mercy and wisdom.

وبعد فتح مكة كان هناك عدد كبير أسرى من قريش، وسألهم
رسول الله: "يا معشر قريش ما ترون أني فاعل بكم؟" فرد الأسرى وكلهم
خوف من انتقام محمد منهم: "خيراً، أخ كريم وإبن أخ كريم"، فقال لهم
رسول الله: "اذهبوا فأنتم الطلقاء"
سبحان الله الذى أنعم على نبيه
الرحمة والحكمة.

In the tenth Hijri year,
the Messenger of Allah performed the obligatory
Hajj for the first and only time in his life.
He delivered an important khutbah (sermon)
which is considered his final advice to all Muslims
until the Day of Judgement.

وفى العام الهجرى العاشر أدى رسول الله فريضة الحج مرة واحدة فى حياته، وألقى
فيها خطبة هامة تعتبر وصيته لجميع المسلمين الى يوم القيامة.

This khutbah included a call to Muslims
to fear and obey Allah.
He warned them of the hatred of Shaytan towards
humans and his plots to push Muslims to commit sin.
The Prophet enjoined goodness towards women,
and caring about each other.
On that day, an important Quranic verse was revealed,
announcing the completion and perfection of the Message.

وتضمنت هذه الخطبة دعوة المسلمين الى تقوى الله وطاعته، ونبه رسول الله
من عداوة الشيطان لبني آدم ومكائده لإيقاعهم في الخطيئة، وقد أوصى
الرسول بالنساء خيراً ورعاية المؤمن لأخيه المؤمن. وفي هذا اليوم أنزل
الله الآية التالية معلناً تمام رسالته لنبيه واكتمال الدين.

"...Today, I have perfected
your religion for you,
and have completed My blessing upon you,
and have chosen for you Islam
as your religion..." (3)
(Al-Maeda)

سُوۡرَةُ المَائدَة

بِسۡمِ اللهِ الرَّحۡمٰنِ الرَّحِیۡمِ

... اَلۡیَوۡمَ اَکۡمَلۡتُ لَکُمۡ دِیۡنَکُمۡ وَاَتۡمَمۡتُ عَلَیۡکُمۡ نِعۡمَتِیۡ وَرَضِیۡتُ لَکُمُ الۡاِسۡلَامَ دِیۡنًا ... ۳

Prophet Muhammad
said at the end of his farewell khutbah during his Hajj:

"And I have left among you that which if you follow it, you will not go astray: the Book of Allah and the Sunnah of His Prophet. Be my witness, O Allah, that I have conveyed your Message to your people."

The Muslims replied: Yes, By Allah, we bear witness that you conveyed the Message and fulfilled the trust, O beloved of Allah.

قال رسول اللّه فى نهاية خطبة الوداع أثناء حجه:

"وإني قد تركت فيكم ما إن أخذتم به لن تضلوا بعده: كتاب الله وسنة نبيه، ألا هل بلغت اللهم فاشهد"

ورد المؤمنون: نعم، اللهم إنا نشهد أنك بلغت الرسالة وأديت الأمانة يا حبيب الله.

In the eleventh year after Hijra,
Muhammad (pbuh) died in Medina at the age of 63 years,
after delivering the Message of Allah over a period of 23 years.
He spent the first thirteen years of them in Makkah,
and continued delivering his Message after his emigration to
Medina until he passed away.

وفى العام الحادى عشر هجرى توفى محمد عليه الصلاة والسلام فى
المدينة المنورة، وكان عمره 63 عاماً بعد أن بلغ رسالة الله على
مدى 23 عاماً قضى منها ثلاثة عشر عاماً فى مكة، وإستمر فى
دعوته بعد هجرته الى المدينة المنورة حتى وافته المنية.

The whole life of Allah's Messenger
Muhammad bin Abdullah peace be upon him,
the Seal of the Prophets and Messengers,
is full of advice and instructions to the Muslim nation.
His actions and words constitute the Sunnah and hadith
of the Prophet, which, together with the Holy Qur'an
represent the path of righteousness and success in this
world and the hereafter.

حياة رسول الله محمد بن عبد الله خاتم الأنبياء والمرسلين عليه الصلاة والسلام
كلها حكم وتعاليم للأمة الإسلامية، فأفعاله وأقواله
تُكوّن السنة النبوية والحديث الشريف، وهذه السنة النبوية
مع القرآن الكريم يمثلان طريق الهداية والنجاح فى الدنيا والآخرة.

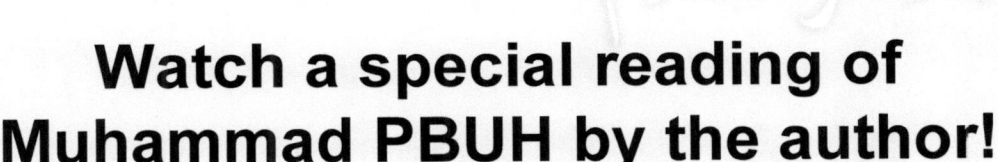

Watch a special reading of Muhammad PBUH by the author!

Scan the QR code to access the video.

www.ingramcontent.com/pod-product-compliance
Lightning Source LLC
Chambersburg PA
CBHW041433120626
46547CB00002B/196